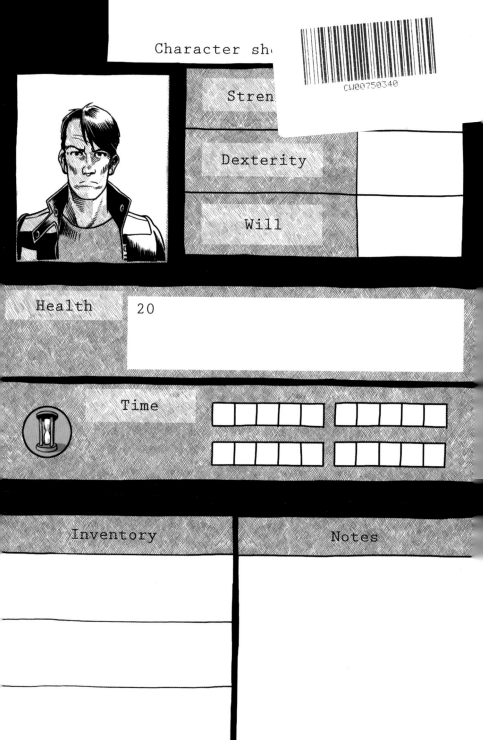

Author: Manuro - Illustrator: MC
This book is a translation of the original *Captive - La BD dont vous êtes le héros*. © Makaka Éditions 2014

Van Ryder Games and Graphic Novel Adventures are Trademarks of Van Ryder Games LLC
ISBN: 978-0-9997698-0-5   Library of Congress Control Number: 2018933572
Published by Van Ryder Games and printed in the USA. Second printing.

Find printable character sheets and the entire collection of Graphic Novel Adventures at www.vanrydergames.com

Captive

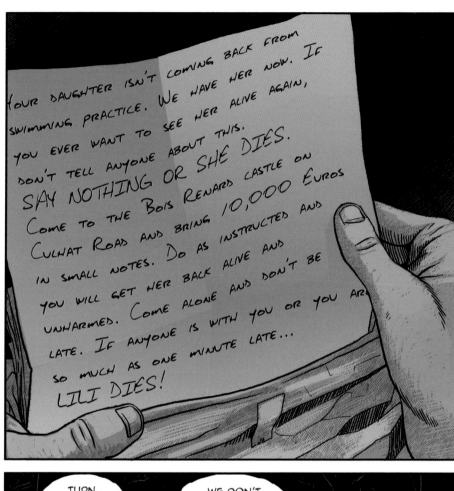

1 | NOW, IT'S YOUR TURN...

WHAT HAPPENS NEXT DEPENDS ON THE CHOICES YOU MAKE. BEFORE YOU BEGIN BE SURE YOU HAVE READ THE GAME RULES AT THE BEGINNING OF THE BOOK AND CREATED YOUR CHARACTER SHEET AS INSTRUCTED. WHEN YOU ARE READY, CHOOSE ONE OF THE TWO DOORS BY TURNING TO FRAME 49 OR 25.

YOU CAN SHOOT THE ANIMAL IN *38* OR STEP BACK AND SHUT THE DOOR BEHIND YOU IN *19*.

A *FLASHLIGHT* THAT WORKS. IT COULD COME IN HANDY. YOU NEVER KNOW. ADD IT TO YOUR *INVENTORY* IF YOU WISH TO TAKE IT WITH YOU.

THEN GO BACK TO *18*.

YOU HAVE YOUR REFLEXES TO THANK FOR THAT. GO TO *43*.

9

READ *ANNEX B* AT THE END OF THE BOOK. ONCE READ, GO TO 27.

10

...

YOU COULD HAVE SWORN THERE WAS SOMETHING THERE. GO TO 6.

11

NO NEED TO WASTE YOUR TIME HERE. BETTER GO BACK TO THE CORRIDOR IN 42.

12

READ **ANNEX C** AT THE END OF THE BOOK. ONCE READ, GO TO 51.

13

GO TO **34** IF YOU HAVE CHOSEN THIS COMBINATION, OR GO TO **46** FOR ANY OTHER CHOICE.

14

15

WHAT A LOT OF USELESS JUNK...

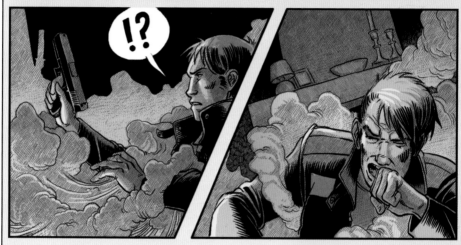

!?

THE SMOKE IS BURNING YOUR LUNGS. LOSE **4 HEALTH.** YOU MUST RUN AWAY AS FAST AS YOU CAN AND YOU WON'T BE ABLE TO RETURN TO THIS ROOM.

49

57

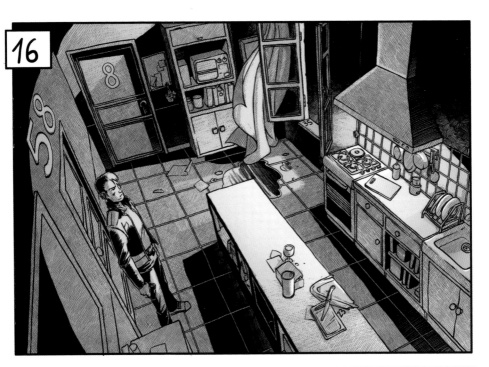

16

17

YOU HAVE FOUND THE RIGHT COMBINATION. THE DOOR IS NOW UNLOCKED AND GIVES YOU ACCESS TO THIS STRANGE ROOM. YOU CAN RUMMAGE THROUGH THIS MESS IN *30* OR RETRACE YOUR STEPS IN *26*.

18

THE ROTTING STENCH IN THIS ROOM IS UNBEARABLE, AS IF YOU HAD JUST OPENED THE DOOR OF A FRIDGE LEFT UNPLUGGED FOR WEEKS, LOADED WITH FOOD. *SICKENING...*

19

THE ANIMAL KILLS YOU AND HERE YOUR ADVENTURE COMES TO A PREMATURE END.

21

BAM

PAK

YOU CAN TAKE SHELTER BEHIND THE POTTED PLANT IN 44...

...OR YOU CAN DIVE TOWARDS THE TABLE WHILST AIMING AND SHOOTING AT YOUR ENEMY AS BEST YOU CAN IN 56.

22

NAKED GIRL VS. DINOSAURS

IT'S SPECTACULAR!

WHAT IS THIS DOING HERE? YOU CAN TAKE THE MAGAZINE AND ADD IT YOUR INVENTORY IF YOU LIKE...

THEN GO BACK TO 27.

23

YOU CAN TAKE THIS BUTCHER'S KNIFE AND ADD IT TO YOUR INVENTORY IF YOU WANT.

THEN GO BACK TO 16.

YOU CAN PULL OPEN THE CURTAIN WITH YOUR GUN DRAWN IN 10 OR DIVE IN TO NEUTRALIZE YOUR POTENTIAL ENEMY IN 66.

YOU SWEAR YOU SAW
SOMETHING MOVING IN
THE TREES... WAS IT
JUST A SHADOW?

YOU CAN EITHER
CHOOSE TO KEEP
LOOKING FOR LILI
INSIDE THE MANOR
AND RETURN THERE
THROUGH THE VERANDA
IN 65 OR YOU CAN
DECIDE TO GO CLOSER
TO THE GAP IN 47.

30

RUMMAGING THROUGH THIS JUNK WAS A WASTE OF TIME.

AS YOU DON'T WANT TO LEAVE EMPTY-HANDED, YOU CAN TAKE THIS LIGHTER AND ADD IT TO YOUR INVENTORY. THE ENGRAVING AT THE FRONT HAS CAUGHT YOUR INTEREST. BESIDES, THIS KIND OF OBJECT CAN ALWAYS COME IN HANDY. THEN GO BACK TO 26.

31

BAM BAM

GO TO 45.

32

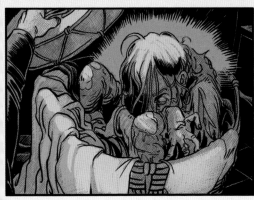

GO TO 49.

YOU CAN'T RETURN TO THIS ROOM.

33

You have a new message

CLOVIS

From: CLOVIS

JEFF'S GONE UPSTAIRS COME ASAP

GO TO 14.

34

YOU CAN'T OPEN THE DOOR AND THE WHEELS WON'T MOVE EITHER. THE MECHANISM MUST BE STUCK.

DAMMIT!

GO BACK TO 26. YOU WON'T BE ABLE TO COME BACK TO THIS DOOR.

BETTER NOT LINGER. THE
MERE THOUGHT OF LILI BEING
LOCKED UP IN THIS KIND OF
ROOM IS BLOODCURDLING.
YOU HAVE TO FIND HER AS
SOON AS POSSIBLE.
GO BACK TO 16.

YOU CAN DIVE AND TAKE SHELTER BEHIND THE POTTED PLANT IN 44 OR SHOOT RIGHT AWAY IN 4.

CLAK

YOU CAN STEP BACK WITH YOUR GUN DRAWN IN 5...

...OR RUN TO THE INTRUDER TO NEUTRALIZE HIM IN 20.

38

THE PAIN FROM THE BITE IS INCREDIBLE AND YOU LOSE 5 HEALTH. GO TO 27.

39

ALL IS QUIET IN THIS ROOM. YOU CAN LEAVE THROUGH ONE OF THE EXITS OR, ALTERNATIVELY, YOU CAN EITHER HAVE A CLOSER LOOK AT THE FIREPLACE IN 15 OR TAKE A GOOD LOOK AROUND THE SITTING-ROOM IN 48.

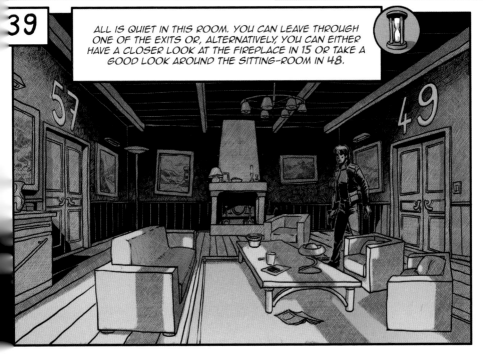

IF YOU'VE BEEN HERE BEFORE, GO DIRECTLY TO 27.

40

GO TO 59 IF YOUR WILL IS 7 OR HIGHER. IF NOT, GO TO 2.

41

THIS IS NO PLACE TO KEEP VINTAGE WINES-- IT'S TOO COLD AND DAMP. THERE'S NO DOUBT ABOUT ONE THING: YOUR DAUGHTER IS HELD CAPTIVE ELSEWHERE. CLIMB BACK UP THROUGH THE TRAPDOOR IN 50.

THE TEMPERATURE HAS SUDDENLY DROPPED. YOUR HEART CAN'T RESIST AND IT STOPS, AS IF SQUEEZED MERCILESSLY BY A FROZEN HAND. LILI WILL NEVER SEE HER FATHER'S FACE AGAIN.

GO TO 17 IF YOU HAVE CHOSEN THIS COMBINATION. GO TO 34 FOR ANY OTHER CHOICE.

YOU STILL HAVE TIME TO TAKE SHELTER IN THE MANOR AT 65. IF YOU PREFER RAISING YOUR GUN WITH TREMBLING HANDS, GO TO 31.

YOU NOW HAVE A CLEARER IDEA OF WHERE THIS MIGHT LEAD YOU... ADD THE YELLOW KEY TO YOUR INVENTORY IF YOU WISH TO KEEP IT. THEN GO BACK TO 43.

52

TURN ON THE LIGHT IF YOU WANT TO SEE MORE CLEARLY AND GO TO 41.

53

54

IT HAPPENS TO BE AN EXCELLENT COGNAC. IT COULD BE A SHOT OF LIQUID COURAGE WHEN YOU NEED IT MOST. YOU CAN ADD THE COGNAC TO YOUR INVENTORY IF YOU WISH. YOU MAY TAKE A SIP AT ANY TIME TO RESTORE 2 HEALTH. THE BOTTLE HAS 2 SIPS LEFT. GO BACK TO 50.

55

IF YOUR DEXTERITY IS LESS THAN OR EQUAL TO 7, YOU MISS A STEP AND FALL DOWN THE STAIRS. LOSE 4 HEALTH.

YOU FEEL AROUND IN THE DARK AND, MUCH TO YOUR RELIEF, FIND A SWITCH. YOU FLIP IT ON. GO TO 41.

56

YOU ARE SERIOUSLY WOUNDED. LOSE 7 HEALTH AND 1 POINT EACH OF STRENGTH, DEXTERITY AND WILL. THEN, GO TO 43.

57

GO STRAIGHT TO 42 IF YOU HAVE BEEN IN THIS CORRIDOR BEFORE. IF NOT, CHECK YOUR TIME VALUE. GO TO 24 IF IT IS GREATER OR EQUAL TO 3. OTHERWISE GO TO 37.

60

YOU CAN CLIMB DOWN THIS STAIRCASE BUT IT SEEMS VERY DARK. GO TO 52 IF YOU HAVE A FLASHLIGHT. IF NOT, YOU CAN TRY YOUR LUCK WITH NO LIGHT IN 55 OR GO BACK TO THE KITCHEN IN 16.

61

IT IS NOT AS GOOD AS A TEAR GAS GRENADE, BUT YOU CAN CHOOSE TO TAKE THIS INSECTICIDE AND ADD IT TO YOUR INVENTORY.

THEN GO BACK TO THE CORRIDOR IN 25.

62

64

THE WHEELS SHOW THREE TYPES OF FOOTPRINTS NEXT TO THREE DIFFERENT ANIMALS. THINK OF THE COMBINATION THAT WILL ENABLE YOU TO UNLOCK THIS DOOR.

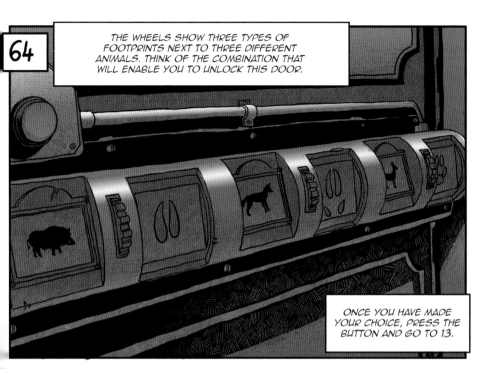

ONCE YOU HAVE MADE YOUR CHOICE, PRESS THE BUTTON AND GO TO 13.

65

YOU NOTICE A *COMPASS* ON THE LOWER TABLE. YOU CAN ADD IT TO YOUR *INVENTORY* IF YOU LIKE.

66

NO ONE HERE. YOU'RE SO NERVOUS THAT YOU LOSE 2 HEALTH AND 1 POINT OF DEXTERITY. GO TO 6.

67

NO SIGN OF YOUR DAUGHTER HERE. YOU'D BETTER GO BACK TO THE CORRIDOR IN 25.

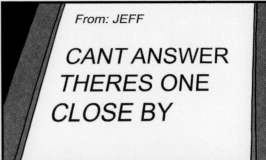

From: JEFF

CANT ANSWER THERES ONE CLOSE BY

BETTER KEEP QUIET.
GO TO 105.

69

YOU CAN'T MISS HIM FROM
WHERE YOU ARE. GO TO 114.

BAM

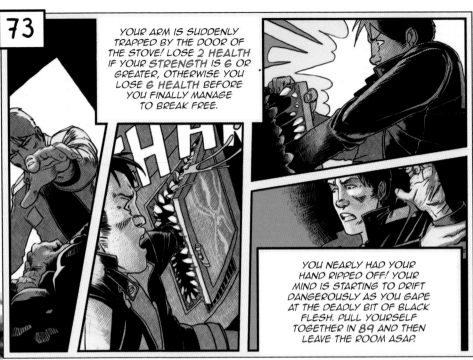

73

YOUR ARM IS SUDDENLY TRAPPED BY THE DOOR OF THE STOVE! LOSE 2 HEALTH IF YOUR STRENGTH IS 6 OR GREATER, OTHERWISE YOU LOSE 6 HEALTH BEFORE YOU FINALLY MANAGE TO BREAK FREE.

YOU NEARLY HAD YOUR HAND RIPPED OFF! YOUR MIND IS STARTING TO DRIFT DANGEROUSLY AS YOU GAPE AT THE DEADLY BIT OF BLACK FLESH. PULL YOURSELF TOGETHER IN 89 AND THEN LEAVE THE ROOM ASAP.

74

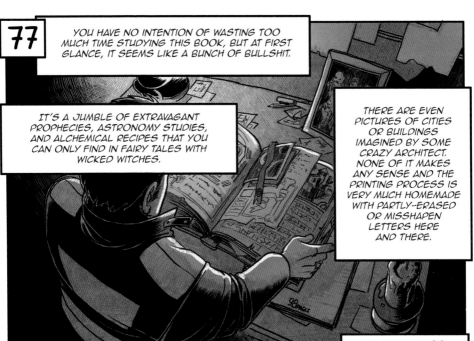

77

YOU HAVE NO INTENTION OF WASTING TOO MUCH TIME STUDYING THIS BOOK, BUT AT FIRST GLANCE, IT SEEMS LIKE A BUNCH OF BULLSHIT.

IT'S A JUMBLE OF EXTRAVAGANT PROPHECIES, ASTRONOMY STUDIES, AND ALCHEMICAL RECIPES THAT YOU CAN ONLY FIND IN FAIRY TALES WITH WICKED WITCHES.

THERE ARE EVEN PICTURES OF CITIES OR BUILDINGS IMAGINED BY SOME CRAZY ARCHITECT. NONE OF IT MAKES ANY SENSE AND THE PRINTING PROCESS IS VERY MUCH HOMEMADE WITH PARTLY-ERASED OR MISSHAPEN LETTERS HERE AND THERE.

GO BACK TO 123.

78

CHIK

YOU CAN WALK DOWN THIS SECRET STAIRCASE IN 120 OR YOU MAY PREFER TO GO BACK TO 111 INSTEAD.

81

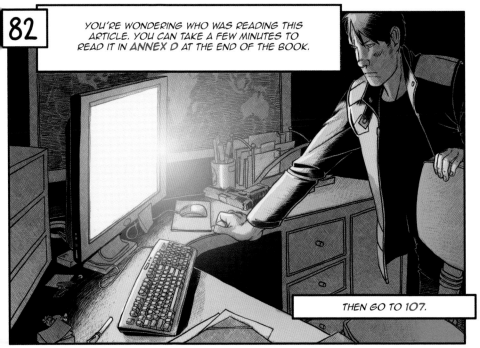

82

YOU'RE WONDERING WHO WAS READING THIS ARTICLE. YOU CAN TAKE A FEW MINUTES TO READ IT IN *ANNEX D* AT THE END OF THE BOOK.

THEN GO TO 107.

83

IT'S USELESS. THE COLLAPSE HAS BLOCKED THE TUNNEL MUCH FARTHER BACK THAN YOU EXPECTED. YOU ARE NOW EXHAUSTED AND FEELING QUITE DISHEARTENED AFTER WASTING SO MUCH TIME.

OK...

...THIS CLEARLY WASN'T A GREAT IDEA.

ONCE YOU'VE REGAINED SOME ENERGY, WALK THROUGH THE ALCOVE ON THE RIGHT IN 102.

84

THEY HAVE KILLED THEM!

MY BABIES...

...MY LITTLE BABIES...

IF YOU WANT TO ASK, "DO YOU KNOW THE MEN WHO DID THIS?", GO TO 97.

IF YOU PREFER TO WAIT FOR HER TO CALM DOWN, GO TO 113.

85

YOU CAN CHOOSE TO TAKE THE GAUZE AND PAINKILLERS AND ADD THEM TO YOUR INVENTORY UNDER "FIRST AID."

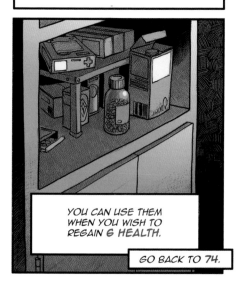

YOU CAN USE THEM WHEN YOU WISH TO REGAIN 6 HEALTH.

GO BACK TO 74.

86

WHY THIS QUESTION?

YOU THINK I'VE LOST MY MIND, DON'T YOU? YOU THINK I'M HALLUCINATING?

GO TO 80 TO ANSWER THIS WAY:

"OF COURSE NOT! I JUST THOUGHT IT STRANGE THAT YOU COULD HEAR IT FROM SO FAR AWAY."

OR GO TO 100 TO ANSWER THIS WAY:

"I DON'T. I JUST WANT TO HELP YOU."

90

YOU'RE RELIEVED YOU WERE ABLE TO TURN OFF THE TAP SO EASILY AND TO HAVE STOPPED THIS DISGUSTING LIQUID FROM POURING INTO THE TUB.

BL.. BLOP

PLOC

YOU CAN UNPLUG THE TUB IN **206** OR MOVE AWAY FROM IT FOR GOOD AND GO BACK TO **74**.

91

I MEAN YOU NO HARM, MADAME MEYRIEU.

I'M A COP. YOU HAVE NOTHING TO WORRY ABOUT ANYMORE.

A COP?

WHY ARE YOU HERE?

...

GO TO **84** TO ANSWER:

"I WANT TO HELP YOU. I CAN GET YOU OUT OF HERE."

IF YOU WANT TO TELL HER ABOUT LILI'S KIDNAPPING AND THE RANSOM, GO TO **80**.

YOU'RE NOW UNARMED AND YOU LOSE 2 HEALTH. YOU CAN FIGHT BACK BY KICKING YOUR OPPONENT AS HARD AS YOU CAN IN 117 OR YOU CAN GRAB HIM AND TRY TO TAKE HIM DOWN IN 109.

93

MAYBE THIS ONE WORKS.

BETTER CHECK IN 79.

94

HE'S DEAD.

YOU FEEL TERRIBLE. IF YOU HADN'T ASKED HIM TO HELP YOU, HE'D STILL BE ALIVE.

AVENGING HIS DEATH DOESN'T MAKE YOU FEEL BETTER.

GO TO 81, WITH A HEAVY HEART.

95

96

A DIARY ON THE FLOOR. YOU DON'T HAVE MUCH TIME, THOUGH.

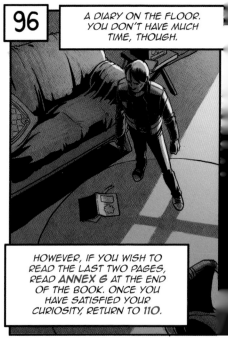

HOWEVER, IF YOU WISH TO READ THE LAST TWO PAGES, READ **ANNEX 6** AT THE END OF THE BOOK. ONCE YOU HAVE SATISFIED YOUR CURIOSITY, RETURN TO 110.

97

HE WAS A SO-CALLED PHOTOGRAPHER.

BUT IN FACT THEY DIDN'T CARE ABOUT THE PHOTOS.

SYLVÈRE MISLEAD US.

...

WHAT DIFFERENCE DOES IT MAKE NOW...

OR HE WAS MISLEAD.

HAD YOU SEEN THEM...

...DOING THEIR WORST. THEY ARE ABSOLUTE *MONSTERS!*

BARBARIC CREATURES, THE *DEVIL'S* SERVANTS!

GO TO *80* TO FIRMLY ASK HER:

"CAN YOU DESCRIBE THEM TO ME?"

OR GO TO *106* TO REASSURE HER AND SAY IN A SOOTHING VOICE:

"YOU'LL BE FINE NOW. THE'RE GONE."

98

HANDWRITTEN NOTES:

YOU GET CHILLS WHEN YOU NOTICE THAT THE HANDWRITING IS EXACTLY THE SAME AS ON THE RANSOM NOTE!

YOU CAN TAKE SOME TIME TO READ THE MOST RECENT PAGES IN *ANNEX F* AT THE END OF THE BOOK. WHEN YOU ARE DONE, GO BACK TO *123*.

99

IF YOU HAVE A *LIGHTER* IN YOUR *INVENTORY*, YOU MAY WANT TO LIGHT THIS OIL LAMP IN *112*.

IF NOT, GO BACK TO *81* TO LEAVE THIS BEDROOM.

IF YOU THINK YOU KNOW THIS WOMAN'S FIRST NAME, MULTIPLY THE NUMBER OF LETTERS IN THE NAME BY THE POSITION IN THE ALPHABET OF THE FIRST LETTER (A = 1, B = 2....). THEN GO TO THE RESULT YOU HAVE OBTAINED.

IF YOU YOU THINK YOU HAVE A BETTER IDEA OF HER LAST NAME, CALCULATE THE RESULT USING THE SAME METHOD AS ABOVE AND GO TO THE RESULT YOU HAVE OBTAINED. IF YOU DO NOT KNOW HER NAME, GO TO 80.

103

THIS DOOR IS LOCKED AND YOU HAVE NO KEY MATCHING THE LOCK.

GO BACK TO 111.

104

STILL VERY MUCH MOVED BY YOUR ENCOUNTER WITH THIS POOR VICTIM, YOU MAKE A MENTAL NOTE TO CALL 911 AS SOON AS YOUR DAUGHTER IS SAFE FROM HER KIDNAPPERS. YOU RETURN TO THE BEDROOM IN 111.

105

THE STAIRS LEADING UP TO THE NEXT FLOOR ARE BARRED BY A PADLOCKED DOOR. IF YOU POSSESS THE KEY WITH THE SCOUBIDOU, YOU CAN GO UP TO 150. THE LABELED KEY WILL ALLOW YOU INTO 136.

MY LITTLE BABIES ☞☜

MY...

...BABIES.

...

GO TO 116 TO CAREFULLY ASK HER:

"ARE YOU SURE THERE ARE NO OTHER SURVIVORS?"

OR GO TO 87 TO SAY:

"LET ME TAKE YOU SOMEWHERE SAFE."

TAK

WHAT WAS *THAT?*

WHATEVER IT WAS, IT APPEARS TO BE GONE. YOU CAN LEAVE THE COMPUTER AND GO BACK TO 202 OR CONTINUE YOUR SEARCH ON THE COMPUTER IN 125.

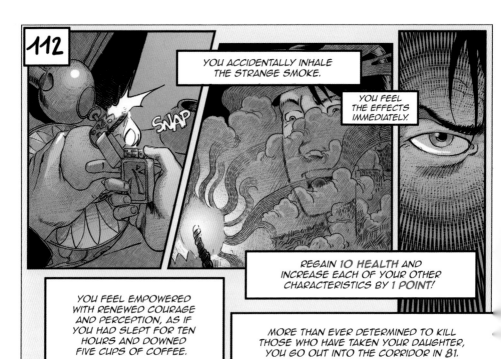

YOU ACCIDENTALLY INHALE THE STRANGE SMOKE.

SNAP

YOU FEEL THE EFFECTS IMMEDIATELY.

REGAIN 10 HEALTH AND INCREASE EACH OF YOUR OTHER CHARACTERISTICS BY 1 POINT!

YOU FEEL EMPOWERED WITH RENEWED COURAGE AND PERCEPTION, AS IF YOU HAD SLEPT FOR TEN HOURS AND DOWNED FIVE CUPS OF COFFEE.

MORE THAN EVER DETERMINED TO KILL THOSE WHO HAVE TAKEN YOUR DAUGHTER, YOU GO OUT INTO THE CORRIDOR IN 81.

113

BUT I'LL AVENGE THEM!

BRING ME...

...THE SICKLE THAT IS IN THE GREENHOUSE.

I'LL MAKE THEM PAY FOR WHAT THEY'VE DONE!

GO AND GET IT FOR ME IF YOU REALLY MEAN TO HELP ME.

CALM DOWN.

I--

I'LL STAB THOSE BASTARDS! I'LL CUT THEM OPEN!

ALL OF THEM!

GO TO 106 TO ANSWER CALMLY:

"I'LL GO, I PROMISE. I'LL GET IT FOR YOU AS SOON AS I CAN."

OR STEP FORWARD TO COMFORT HER IN 80.

GO TO 75 IF YOUR TIME VALUE IS LESS THAN OR EQUAL TO 4 OR GO TO 94 IF IT IS GREATER.

IN THE DARKNESS YOU BANG YOUR KNEE HARD AGAINST A TABLE. LOSE 1 HEALTH.

BLANG

MAYBE YOU CAN AVOID FURTHER INJURY BY TURNING ON THIS LAMP WHEN YOU GO TO 79.

HAAAAA AAAAA...

BASTARD!

YOU'LL PAY FOR THIS!

YOU CAN LEAP ONTO YOUR OPPONENT IN 71 OR TRY TO PICK UP YOUR GUN IN 88.

KEEP CALM. THE PERSON WHO DID THIS CAN'T BE FAR.

YOU CAN PRESS YOUR BACK AGAINST THE WALL AND WAIT FOR SOMEONE TO APPEAR IN 69 OR CHECK ON CLOVIS, KEEPING AN EYE ON THE HALLWAY IN 63.

THE DOOR IS LOCKED AND YOU DO NOT HAVE A KEY THAT WILL OPEN IT.

CLAC

GO BACK TO 81.

120

IF YOU ARE NOT MISTAKEN, YOU HAVE REACHED THE GROUND FLOOR.

BUT THE STAIRCASE CONTINUES DOWN FURTHER.

POINTLESS AS IT MAY SEEM, YOU CAN TRY TO CLEAR AWAY THE RUBBLE BLOCKING THE WAY ON THE LEFT IN 83, OR KEEP WALKING ALONG THE CORRIDOR ON THE RIGHT IN 102.

121

YOU CAN HELP ME!

COME BACK TO ME FOR CHRIST'S SAKE!

...

IT WON'T BE ENOUGH TO BRING HER BACK TO HER SENSES. BY THE LOOK OF IT, SHE HAS BUT A FEW HOURS TO LIVE. YOU REALLY CAN'T HELP HER AT THIS STAGE. GO BACK TO WHERE YOU CAME FROM IN 104.

122

THEY ARE BIGGER THAN THE WHITE AND RED ONES USED ON THE BUMPER POOL TABLE YOU AND CLOVIS USE WHEN YOU GO TO THE BAR ON THE WEEKENDS.

TAKE THE *BILLIARD BALL* AND ADD IT TO YOUR *INVENTORY*. THEN GO BACK TO *202*.

123

GO BACK TO 111 WHEN YOU FEEL YOU HAVE WASTED ENOUGH TIME...

...OR ONCE YOUR CURIOSITY HAS BEEN SATISFIED.

124

IT SMELLS VAGUELY LIKE GASOLINE.

BUT YOU WOULD NEVER WANT TO FILL UP YOUR TANK WITH IT.

THE FAUCET BEGINS TO POUR EVEN THOUGH YOU HAVEN'T TOUCHED IT!

YOU CAN TRY TO TURN OFF THE TAP IN *90*, OR LEAVE THE BATHROOM IMMEDIATELY IN *74*.

125

NOTHING HELPFUL IN THE INBOX, ESPECIALLY SINCE IT'S FULL OF SPAM.

IN ANY CASE, THERE'S NOTHING THAT SEEMS REMOTELY CONNECTED TO LILI.

TAK

TAK

THIS TIME YOU'RE SURE...

...THERE'S SOMETHING OUTSIDE THE WINDOW!

YOU CAN GO CLOSER TO THE WINDOW TO INVESTIGATE IN 76 OR CHOOSE A DOOR IN 202 IF YOU WISH TO LEAVE.

126

IT LOOKS LIKE A BELL.

THOUGHT IT IS LOCATED A BIT TOO LOW TO BE USED TO CALL THE SERVANTS.

CLIC

CLAC

THERE'S A TINY KEY HOLE.

IF YOU HAVE THE YELLOW KEY YOU CAN INSERT IT IN THE LOCK IN 78.

IF NOT, YOU ATTEMPT TO PICK THE LOCK BUT WITH NO SUCCESS. RETURN TO 111 AND ATTEMPT TO FORGET YOUR FRUSTRATION.

NO ONE THERE!
YOU'RE EITHER TIRED
OR YOU'RE LOSING IT.

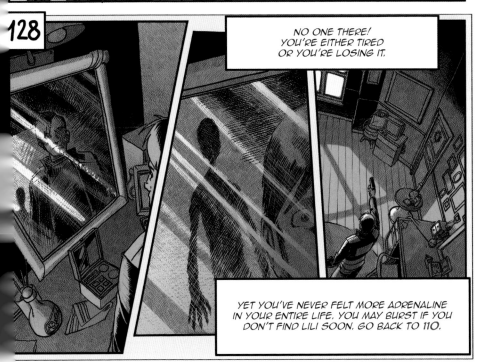

YET YOU'VE NEVER FELT MORE ADRENALINE
IN YOUR ENTIRE LIFE. YOU MAY BURST IF YOU
DON'T FIND LILI SOON. GO BACK TO 110.

132

YOU SHOULD NEVER HAVE HESITATED AGAINST SUCH A VICIOUS OPPONENT.

HE HAS FATALLY WOUNDED YOU. YOUR LAST FEW BREATHS ON THIS EARTH ARE INCREDIBLY PAINFUL.

133

SOLANGE?

DON'T BE AFRAID. I MEAN YOU NO HARM.

SHE SEEMS TO RELAX A BIT AT THE SOUND OF HER NAME.

GO TO 84.

134

GO IMMEDIATELY TO 43 IF YOU HAVE BEEN HERE BEFORE.

IF NOT, CHECK HOW MUCH TIME YOU HAVE LEFT. GO TO 21 IF YOUR *TIME* VALUE IS GREATER THAN OR EQUAL TO 2. OTHERWISE, GO TO 36.

WHAT KIND OF MONSTER COULD
HAVE DONE SUCH A THING? IF
YOU HAVE A WILL OF 6 OR
GREATER, YOU DISCOVER THE
COURAGE TO REMOVE THIS
HORROR FROM THE STOVE
IN 73. IF YOUR WILL IS LESS
THAN 6 OR YOU SIMPLY
PREFER TO LEAVE IT ALONE,
GO BACK TO 89.

138

201   158

139

YOU'RE STUNNED WHEN YOU SEE THE BOOK'S COVER. THE FIRST TIME YOU SAW THIS DRAWING WAS BY YOUR UNCLE'S DEATHBED, WHEN HE HANDED YOU THE SIGNET RING YOU'RE STILL WEARING TODAY. A FAMILY HEIRLOOM YOU HAD PROMISED TO NEVER PART WITH.

YOU HAD FOUND THE STRANGE ENGRAVING ON THE JEWEL UNIQUE AND, UNTIL THIS MOMENT, YOU HAD NEVER SEEN IT ELSEWHERE.

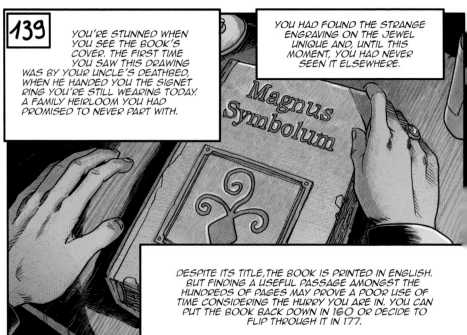

Magnus Symbolum

DESPITE ITS TITLE, THE BOOK IS PRINTED IN ENGLISH. BUT FINDING A USEFUL PASSAGE AMONGST THE HUNDREDS OF PAGES MAY PROVE A POOR USE OF TIME CONSIDERING THE HURRY YOU ARE IN. YOU CAN PUT THE BOOK BACK DOWN IN **160** OR DECIDE TO FLIP THROUGH IT IN **177**.

141

WHAT JUST HAPPENED? YOU CAN'T AFFORD TO LOSE YOUR HEAD NOW!

REMOVE THE **BUTCHER'S KNIFE** FROM YOUR INVENTORY. GO TO 178.

142

THERE IS NO WAY YOU'RE SETTING FOOT IN THAT PSYCHOTIC ZOO AGAIN! GO TO 137.

143

IF YOU'VE SEEN ENOUGH, YOU CAN SWITCH OFF THE TV IN 157...

...OR YOU CAN KEEP WATCHING IN 189.

SHOO!

GET OFF!

SPLAT

YOU LOSE *2 HEALTH.*

THE REPTILE SHOULD LEAVE YOU ALONE NOW, BUT IT DEFINITELY LEFT A MARK.

GO TO *159.*

UNFORTUNATELY THE WRITING ON THE LABEL HAS BEEN ERASED. YOU CAN ADD THIS *LABELED KEY* TO YOUR *INVENTORY.* THEN GO BACK TO *89.*

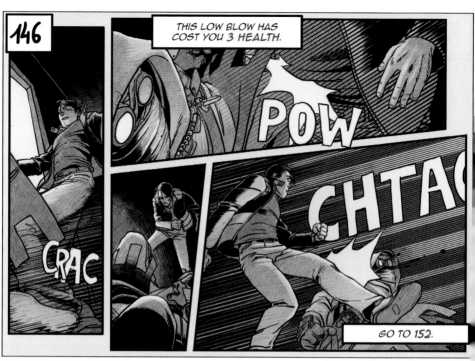

148 AN OPENING INTO THE ATTIC.

YOU CAN TAKE A CLOSER LOOK AT IT IN 169.

149

YOU CAN'T EFFICIENTLY AIM IN THESE CONDITIONS! LOSE 1 HEALTH AS THE SNAKE WRAPS ITSELF AROUND YOU.

SHHH

YOU CAN GRIP THE SNAKE BEHIND ITS HEAD WITH BOTH HANDS IN 174 OR FEEL IN THE DARK FOR SOMETHING TO DEFEND YOURSELF WITH IN 185.

150

GO TO 186 IF YOU HAVE A *BUTCHER'S KNIFE* OR TO 178 IF NOT.

152

NO REASON TO WASTE ANY MORE TIME IN THIS BASTARD'S HIDEOUT.

GO BACK TO THE CORRIDOR IN 201.

153

EITHER THE SWTICH NO LONGER WORKS OR THE BULB HAS BURNT OUT.

GO TO 197 IF YOU'RE DISCOVERING THIS ROOM FOR THE FIRST TIME.

OTHERWISE, GO TO 142.

154

GO TO 204.

155

YOU GOT OUT OF THAT HELL
HOLE ALIVE, WHICH IS QUITE
A FEAT. GO BACK TO 137.

156

YOU WOULD PROBABLY HAVE SUCCEEDED IF
YOUR ENEMY WASN'T SO POWERFUL. YOU
DIDN'T EXPECT THAT KIND OF ATTACK AND YOU
HAVE PAID THE ULTIMATE PRICE. AT LEAST YOU
DIDN'T SUFFER TOO MUCH...

CLiC

CLiC
CLiC

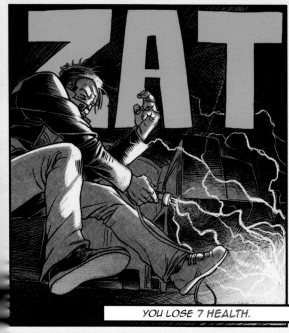

ZAT

YOU LOSE 7 HEALTH.

IF YOU'RE STILL ALIVE, TAKE A MOMENT TO RECOVER...

...BEFORE HEADING FOR 167.

158

IF YOU'RE DISCOVERING THIS ROOM FOR THE FIRST TIME, TO GO 165.

OTHERWISE, EXIT THROUGH ONE OF THE DOORS.

159

KRR...

PLING

!

WHAT WAS THAT? INVESTIGATE IN 129 OR WALK BACK CAREFULLY TO THE DOOR IN 182.

160

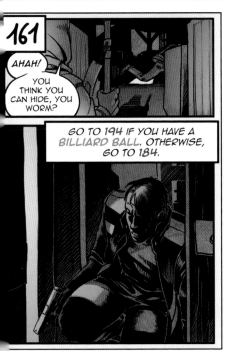

161

AHAH! YOU THINK YOU CAN HIDE, YOU WORM?

GO TO 194 IF YOU HAVE A *BILLIARD BALL*. OTHERWISE, GO TO 184.

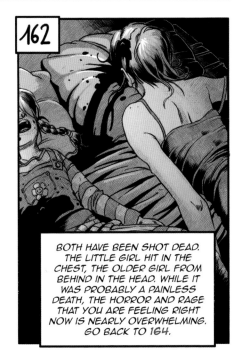

162

BOTH HAVE BEEN SHOT DEAD. THE LITTLE GIRL HIT IN THE CHEST, THE OLDER GIRL FROM BEHIND IN THE HEAD. WHILE IT WAS PROBABLY A PAINLESS DEATH, THE HORROR AND RAGE THAT YOU ARE FEELING RIGHT NOW IS NEARLY OVERWHELMING. GO BACK TO 164.

NO

NO

NO

THANK GOD. IT'S NOT LILI. THERE'S NO DENYING THE FACT THAT YOU'RE RELIEVED...

..BUT YOU CAN'T HELP BUT FEEL HORRIFIED.

YOU CAN LEAVE THIS ROOM THROUGH ONE OF THE DOORS YOU CAN SEE IN THE FIRST PANEL...

...OR YOU CAN FIND THE COURAGE TO EXAMINE THE DEAD BODIES MORE CLOSELY IN *162*.

166

PSCHHHH

PSCHHH

THE FUMES MAKE IT IMPOSSIBLE TO BREATHE. GOOD THING YOU WEREN'T PLANNING ON STAYING.

GO TO 155.

167

201

158

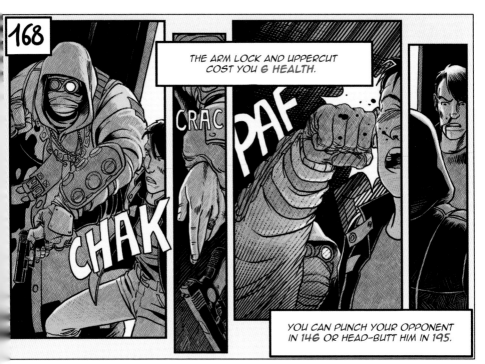

168

THE ARM LOCK AND UPPERCUT COST YOU 6 HEALTH.

CRAC

PAF

CHAK

YOU CAN PUNCH YOUR OPPONENT IN 146 OR HEAD-BUTT HIM IN 195.

169

YOU HEAR FAINT NOISES FROM THE ATTIC. IT SOUNDS LIKE FOOTSTEPS BUT YOU CAN'T BE CERTAIN.

YOU CAN CLIMB UP THE LADDER IN 183 OR CONTINUE TO EXPLORE THE SECOND FLOOR IN 148.

170

GO BACK TO 137.

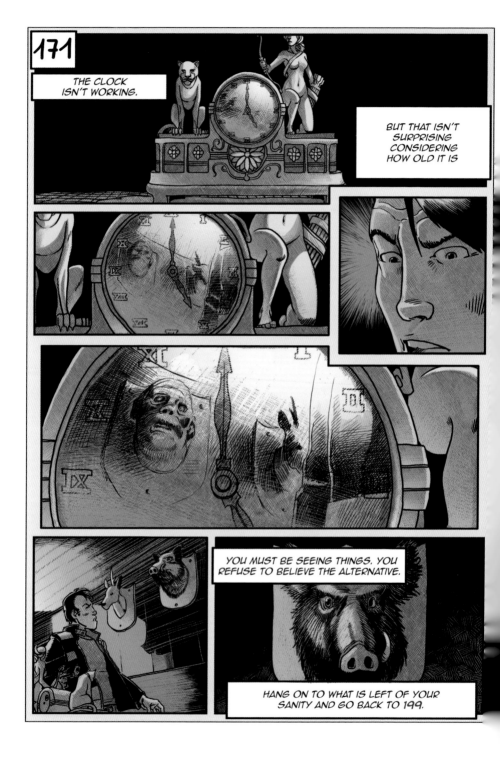

172 IT'S EITHER LOCKED OR STUCK. IF YOU HAVE A KEY, IT WON'T WORK. DON'T BOTHER. BETTER, GO BACK TO 181.

173

SPLAT

HAAAAAAAA

GO TO 152.

174 THE SNAKE TRIES TO OVERPOWER YOU. IT IS INCREDIBLY STRONG.

IF YOUR **STRENGTH** IS LESS THAN OR EQUAL TO 8, YOU LOSE 5 HEALTH. GO TO 151.

175 YOU'LL BE TOO EXPOSED IF YOU KEEP GOING IN THAT DIRECTION.

BETTER GO BACK AND AVOID THIS BASTARD IN 161.

176

YOU LOSE 5 HEALTH.

AAA

THE PAIN CLOUDS YOUR THOUGHTS, WHICH IS PROBABLY FOR THE BEST CONSIDERING WHAT JUST HAPPENED.

REMOVE THE **BUTCHER'S KNIFE** FROM YOUR **INVENTORY** AND GO TO 178.

177

FINALLY, SOMETHING WORTH READING AMIDST ALL THAT MAD SCIENTIST'S BULLSHIT.

HOW TO USE ENTROPY SIGNS IN SACRED THAUMATURGY.

READ ANNEX E AT THE END OF THE BOOK. THEN GO BACK TO 160.

178 158

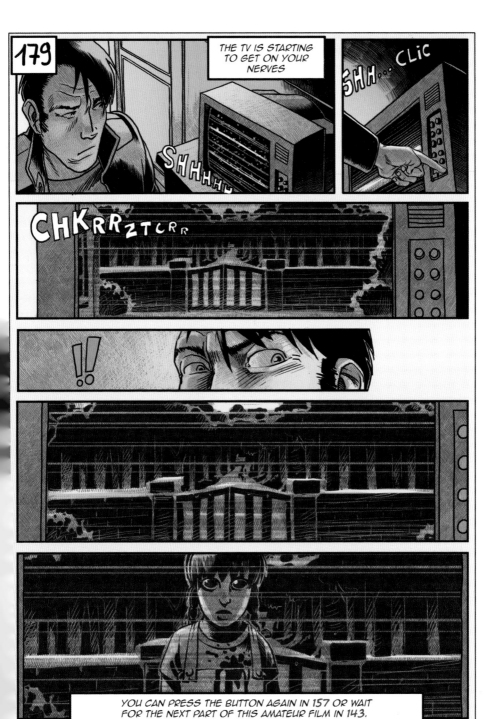

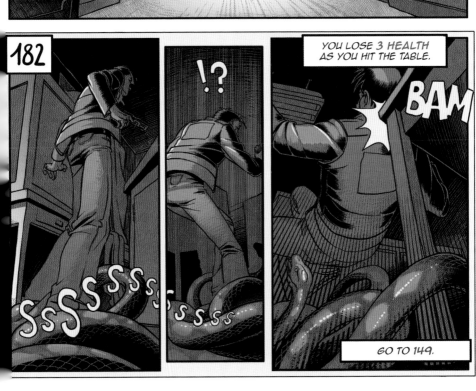

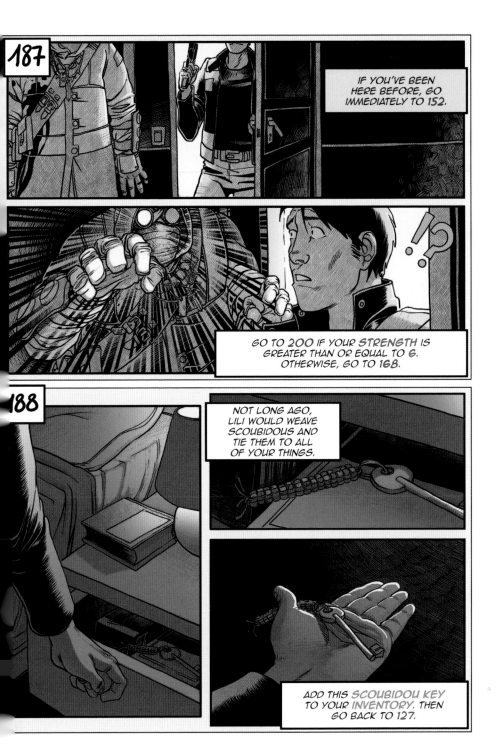

189

GO TO 167.

190

YOU'VE LOST 2 HEALTH
BUT HAVE MANAGED
TO NEUTRALIZE
YOUR ENEMY.

GO TO 163.

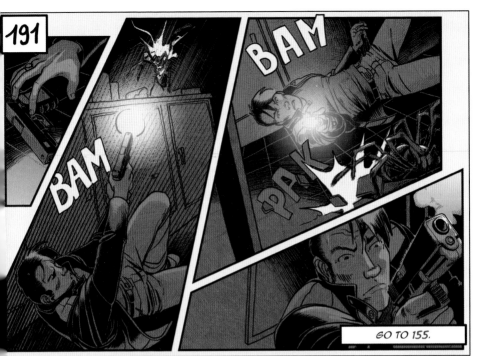

GO TO 155.

IF YOU HAVE A FLASHLIGHT YOU CAN HOLD IT UP AND TRY TO BLIND THIS LUNATIC IN 156.

YOU MAY THINK IT WISER TO SNEAK CLOSER TO HIM IN THE DARK IN 190.

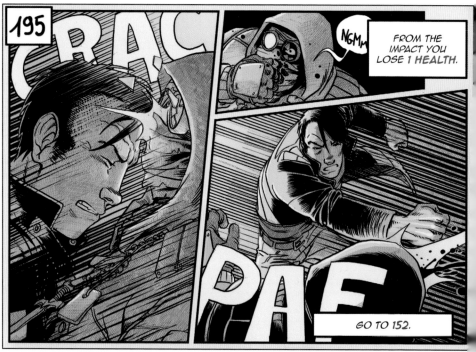

195

NGMM

FROM THE IMPACT YOU LOSE 1 HEALTH.

GO TO 152.

196

YOU LOSE 8 HEALTH.

THE HORRIBLE SMELL OF BURNT FLESH MAKES YOU CHOKE. IT FEELS AS IF YOU ARE BEING SPRAYED WITH BOILING OIL.

GO TO 204.

IN THE DARK WITH THE WIND BLOWING, YOU CAN NEITHER SEE NOR HEAR YOUR ENEMY.

BAM

GO TO 268.

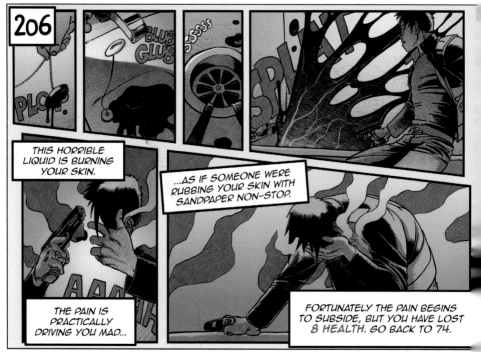

207

BAM

BAM

AN EFFECTIVE TACTIC, BUT YOU'D BETTER NOT STICK AROUND. THE GUNSHOT MAY HAVE BEEN HEARD BY HIS ACCOMPLICES. GO TO 269.

208

210

211

209

DESPITE YOUR BEST EFFORTS, YOU'RE UNABLE TO FIND ANYTHING USEFUL IN THE GREENHOUSE, NOT TO MENTION THE FACT THAT THE BIRDS IN THE CAGE ARE BECOMING MORE AGITATED BY THE MINUTE. YOU CAN SET THEM FREE IN 225 OR GO BACK TO 227 TO LEAVE THE GREENHOUSE.

210

THE PATH APPEARS TO FOLLOW THE WALL BEHIND THE GARDEN BEFORE BENDING BACK TOWARDS THE MANOR. AS FOR THE TRACK BEYOND THE GATE, WHO KNOWS WHERE IT MIGHT LEAD TO?

211

IF YOU'VE BEEN HERE BEFORE, GO TO 205.

212

YOU BARELY ESCAPE...
THAT WAS TOO CLOSE
FOR COMFORT!

GO TO *268*.

213

YOU MAY INVESTIGATE
THIS TRASHED ROOM
IN *241* IF YOU WISH.

UNBELIEVABLE! NOTHING MOVES, SO YOU HAVE BOTH WASTED PRECIOUS TIME AS WELL AS THE ELEMENT OF SURPRISE.

GO BACK TO 252, BEARING IN MIND YOU WILL NOT BE ABLE TO RETURN TO THIS GARAGE.

215

THIS IS THE FIRST TIME ALL NIGHT THAT SOMEONE (OR THING) IS NOT TRYING TO KILL YOU.

IT'S JUST A DOG KENNEL, AND BY THE LOOK OF IT, LILI IS NOT HERE. GO BACK TO 252.

216

YOU HAVE NO RATIONAL EXPLANATION FOR HOW HE DIED. HIS CORPSE SENDS SHIVERS DOWN YOUR SPINE.

LEAVE THE KITCHEN BY GOING BACK TO 213.

217

GO TO 256.

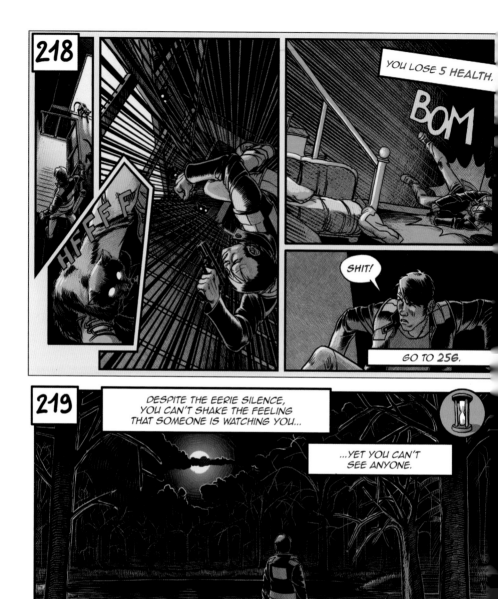

222

YOU CAN'T SEE STRAIGHT.

YOU CAN'T THINK STRAIGHT.

YOU BODY REFUSES TO MOVE.

GO TO 45.

223

POWERLESS, ALL YOU CAN DO IS CRY OUT IN DISTRESS.

BAM
BAM
BAM

GO TO 45.

224

IT'S LILI!

GO TO 246 IF YOU WISH TO ACT NOW OR GO TO 270 IF YOU'D RATHER WAIT FOR A MORE OPPORTUNE MOMENT

225

FLAP FLAP FLAP

CLAC

TRIII

FLAP TRIII

TRIII

YOU LOSE 2 HEALTH.

YOU NEARLY LOST AN EYE! THE NOISE FROM THE BIRDS IS SO LOUD THAT THERE'S NO REASON TO SNEAK ANY LONGER.

FLAP TRIII TRIII

LEAVE IN 227 AND CONTINUE YOUR INVESTIGATION IN THE GARDEN.

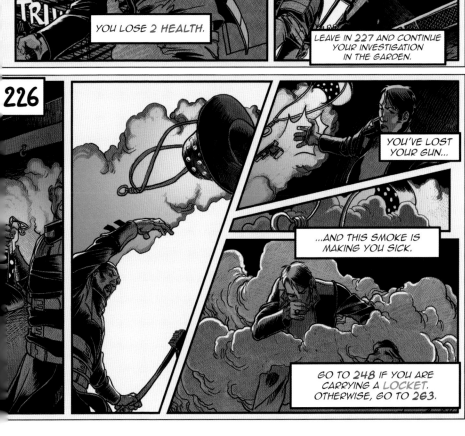

226

YOU'VE LOST YOUR GUN...

...AND THIS SMOKE IS MAKING YOU SICK.

GO TO 248 IF YOU ARE CARRYING A LOCKET. OTHERWISE, GO TO 263.

227

YOU AVOID THE LIGHT SWITCH. LIGHTING UP THE GREENHOUSE WOULD BE AS SUBTLE AS HOOTING IN THE MIDDLE OF THE COURTYARD.

HOWEVER, YOU CAN GROPE YOUR WAY THROUGH THE DARKNESS IN 233...

...OR TURN ON A **FLASHLIGHT** IN 266 IF YOU HAVE ONE.

IF YOU PREFER TO LEAVE, GO TO 268 OR 255.

228

IF YOU WISH TO SEE WHERE THIS TRAPDOOR LEADS TO, GO TO 239 IF YOUR **TIME** VALUE IS LESS THAN OR EQUAL TO 10. IF IT IS GREATER, GO TO 272.

IF NOT, GO BACK TO 215.

229

BAM

THE HUNTED IS NOW THE HUNTER!

YOU CAN EITHER TAKE SHELTER BEHIND THE BUSH IN 207 OR RETURN FIRE AS BEST YOU CAN IN 261.

230

YOU LOSE 1 HEALTH.

FORTUNATELY, YOU MANAGED TO FREE YOURSELF FROM THIS LEAFY TRAP.

RETURN TO 268.

231

GO TO 213.

232

CLiC

YOU LOSE
6 HEALTH.

CHTAK

IF YOU'RE STILL ALIVE,
YOU SWEAR YOU'LL GET
REVENGE ON THE SICK
BASTARD WHO SET THIS
TRAP. ENTER THE HUT IN 221.

233

THE BIRDS ARE STARTING TO GET
AGITATED AS YOU APPROACH. YOU
CAN OPEN THE DOOR OF THE CAGE
IN 225, CAREFULLY EXAMINE THE
REST OF THE GREENHOUSE IN 209,
OR LEAVE BY GOING BACK TO 227.

236

YOU LOSE 4 HEALTH.

YOU CAN ESCAPE DOWN THE STAIRS IN 218 OR SHOOT AT ONE OF THOSE MONSTROUS CREATURES IN 240.

237

NEGO

CHLARRISSKIA

KARVALA

THE ANCIENT BOOK MENTIONED A SPECIFIC BODY PART. ADD UP THE VALUE OF THE LETTERS IT CONTAINS BY REFERRING TO THEIR POSITION IN THE ALPHABET (A=1, B=2...). THEN GO TO THE RESULT YOU HAVE OBTAINED. IF THE RESULT DOESN'T MAKE SENSE, GO TO 276.

238

A RATHER BASIC WEAPON, BUT UNDOUBTEDLY QUITE EFFECTIVE IN MELEE COMBAT.

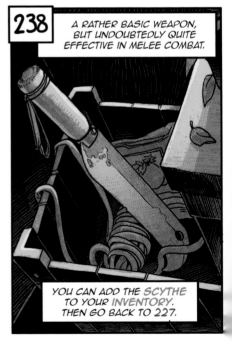

YOU CAN ADD THE SCYTHE TO YOUR INVENTORY. THEN GO BACK TO 227.

240

BAM

YOU'VE KILLED IT. YOU CAN GUN DOWN ANOTHER ONE OF THESE DISGUSTING CATS IN 220 OR ESCAPE DOWN THE STAIRS IN 256.

241

YOU JUST SPEND SEVERAL MINUTES LOOKING FOR ANY KIND OF CLUE OR USEFUL ITEM IN THIS MESS. BUT IT WAS A WASTE OF TIME.

GO BACK TO 213.

242

YOU RESIST THE URGE TO PUT A BULLET IN THAT LUNATIC'S HEAD, BECAUSE WHO KNOWS WHAT MIGHT HAPPEN TO LILI. SHE MUST BE CLOSE BY...

...YOU CAN FEEL IT IN YOUR BONES.

GO TO 274 TO CAREFULLY ENTER THE PASSAGE ON THE LEFT...

...OR GO TO 224 TO STUDY THIS VILLAIN LONGER.

243 IF YOU HAVE BEEN IN THIS GARDEN BEFORE, GO BACK TO **268**.

YOU LOSE 1 HEALTH.

THE WIND IS WEAKER BEHIND THESE HEDGES. YOU LISTEN CAREFULLY, IN CASE YOUR DAUGHTER MAY BE CALLING FOR HELP.

GO TO **230** IF YOUR **STRENGTH** IS GREATER THAN OR EQUAL TO **8**. OTHERWISE, GO TO **259**.

244

275

260

210

245

BLUB
BLUB

GO TO 265 IF YOUR WILL IS
GREATER THAN OR EQUAL TO 6.
OTHERWISE, GO TO 222.

246

GO TO 234 IF YOU HAVE A *SCYTHE* OR GO TO 278 IF YOU HAVE A *BUTCHER'S KNIFE*.

IF YOU DO NOT HAVE A WEAPON, GO TO 273 IF YOU HAVE WRITTEN THE CODE "LIBERATION". OTHERWISE, GO TO 226.

247

BAM

AAA

THE SHOT FROM BEHIND CAUSES YOU TO LOSE 7 HEALTH.

BAM
BAM
BAM

FORTUNATELY FOR YOU, THE GUNMAN MUST BE AN AMATEUR. GO TO 208.

248

FSH

YOU CAN FEEL THE LOCKET HEAT UP AGAINST YOUR SKIN.

YOU CAN DODGE THE MAN'S ASSAULT IN 235 OR HOLD OUT THE LOCKET IN FRONT OF YOU IN 253.

249

THAT WASN'T VERY DISCREET.

YOU CAN HIDE UNTIL THEY CALM DOWN AND COME BACK IN 252...

...OR YOU CAN REOPEN THE DOOR AND GO INTO THE KENNEL IN 215.

250

YOU'VE BECOME PLANT FOOD. THE GARDEN WILL BE YOUR TOMB AS YOU SLOWLY BECOME FERTILIZER.

251

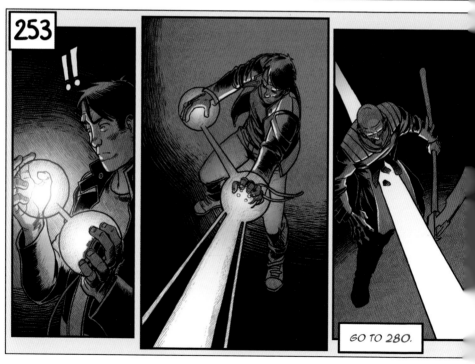

GO TO 280.

YOU THINK YOU'D BE USED TO SEEING DEAD BODIES BY NOW. INSTEAD, YOU CAN FEEL THE PANIC BUILDING INSIDE OF YOUR CHEST.

HOWEVER, YOU CAN CHOOSE TO HAVE A CLOSER LOOK AT THE BODY IN *216* OR LEAVE THE KITCHEN IMMEDIATELY AND RETURN TO *213*.

255

256

GO TO *252*. YOU WON'T BE ABLE TO RETURN TO THIS HOUSE AGAIN.

257

GO TO 246 IF YOUR *TIME* VALUE IS LESS THAN OR EQUAL TO 12. OTHERWISE, GO TO 226.

258

YOU COULD HAVE SWORN THAT YOU HEARD S--

THE GUNSHOT MAY HAV BEEN HEARD BY HIS FRIENDS, IF HE HAS AN LEFT. YOU'RE AT RISK IF YOU STAY HERE ANY LONGER. GO TO 205.

SUDDENTLY, THE PLANT LOOSENS ITS GRIP... *ACT NOW!*

GO TO 212 IF YOUR STRENGTH IS GREATER THAN OR EQUAL TO 7. OTHERWISE, GO TO 250.

YOU'RE BEING CUT TO RIBBONS BY THE VINE'S THORNS AND YOU LOSE 3 HEALTH.

261

YOUR MOONLIT WALK THROUGH THE GARDEN TURNS OUT TO BE DEADLY. DEFEATED, YOU CAN ONLY HOPE THAT YOUR KILLER WILL MAKE YOUR DEATH A QUICK ONE.

262

IF YOU HAVE A LIGHTER, YOU'RE TEMPTED TO SET FIRE TO THE VEHICLES. THAT MIGHT DRAW LILI'S KIDNAPPERS INTO THE OPEN.

LIGHT UP THE NIGHT IN 214...

...OR DECIDE TO LOOK ELSEWHERE IN 252.

263

YOU'RE NOT JUST FEELING SICK...

...IT'S AS IF HIS GAZE HAS MADE YOUR BOWELS DRY UP.

YOU NO LONGER HAVE CONTROL OVER YOUR BODY.

YOU BEGIN TO WALK TOWARDS LILI...

DAD?

...WITH THE HORRIBLE REALIZATION THAT YOU HAVE BECOME A MERE PUPPET IN THE HANDS OF A MAD PUPPET MASTER.

GO TO 237 IF YOU HAVE WRITTEN THE CODE "NEGO" OR GO TO 276 IF YOU HAVE NOT.

264

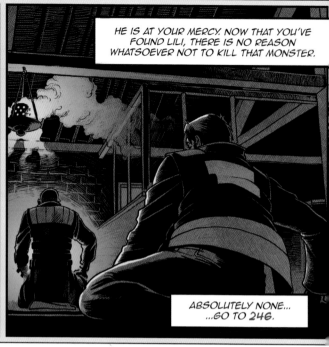

HE IS AT YOUR MERCY. NOW THAT YOU'VE FOUND LILI, THERE IS NO REASON WHATSOEVER NOT TO KILL THAT MONSTER.

ABSOLUTELY NONE...
...GO TO 246.

265

THIS DEFIES ALL RATIONAL EXPLANATION, BUT WHAT IS QUITE CERTAIN IS THAT YOU ARE IN GRAVE DANGER.

YOU CAN EITHER SHOOT IN 223 OR ESCAPE INTO THE WOODS IN 251.

266

THE NOISE WILL GIVE YOU AWAY!

YOU MUST LEAVE AS SOON AS YOU CAN IF YOU DON'T WANT YOUR ENEMIES TO FIND YOU HERE. RETURN TO 227 AND CONTINUE YOUR SEARCH IN THE GARDEN.

267

ALL THINGS CONSIDERED, THIS FLOOR IS PROBABLY NOT WORTH YOUR TIME. YOU CAN GO BACK DOWNSTAIRS IN 217 OR WALK EAGERLY TOWARDS THE CAT IN 236.

268

YOU'VE SEEN ENOUGH. YOU CAN'T STAND HERE AND DO NOTHING. GO TO 226.

YOU CAN GO BACK TO 260 IF YOU DON'T FEEL LIKE CRAWLING.

GO TO 257.

273

DAD?!

GIVE UP!

THERE'S NOTHING YOU CAN DO TO DEFEAT ME.

LILI, STAY WHERE YOU ARE!

PRAY TO YOUR GOD, GUARDIAN...

GO TO **235**.

..AND HOPE HE CAN SAVE YOUR SOUL!

274

GO TO **239**.

275

YOU HAVE BEEN FOLLOWING THIS PATH FOR THE PAST FIVE MINUTES. THE CRACKING OF THE BRANCHES UNDER YOUR FEET SEEMS TO VIOLATE THE SURROUNDING SILENCE.

I SAW THAT AS WELL.

YOU CAME TO MY HOUSE WITH TWO OTHER MEN.

ARE THEY YOUR FRIENDS?

YES, THEY'RE WITH ME.

WE CAME HERE TO FIND MY DAUGHTER...

...DO YOU KNOW WHERE SHE IS?

...

ONE OF YOUR FRIENDS, THE OLDEST WITH THE BEARD...

...HE IS NEARBY.

GO TO 193.

YOU FOUND MY KNIFE, IT WOULD SEEM.

YOU LEAVE THIS BITTER WORLD FULL OF QUESTIONS AND WONDERING WHAT JUST HAPPENED.

COME ON.

LET'S GO.

YOU'VE BOTH SURVIVED THIS HELL.

YOUR CELL PHONE, HOWEVER, WASN'T AS LUCKY.

UNABLE TO CALL FOR BACKUP OR EMERGENCY SERVICES, YOU YET AGAIN...

...HAVE ONLY YOURSELF TO RELY ON.

THE END

Manuro

WELL DONE! IF YOU WISH TO ASSESS YOUR OVERALL SCORE FOR THIS ADVENTURE, CONSULT THE LIST OF ACHIEVEMENTS AT THE END OF THE BOOK.

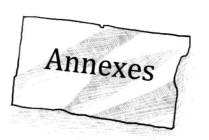

Annexes

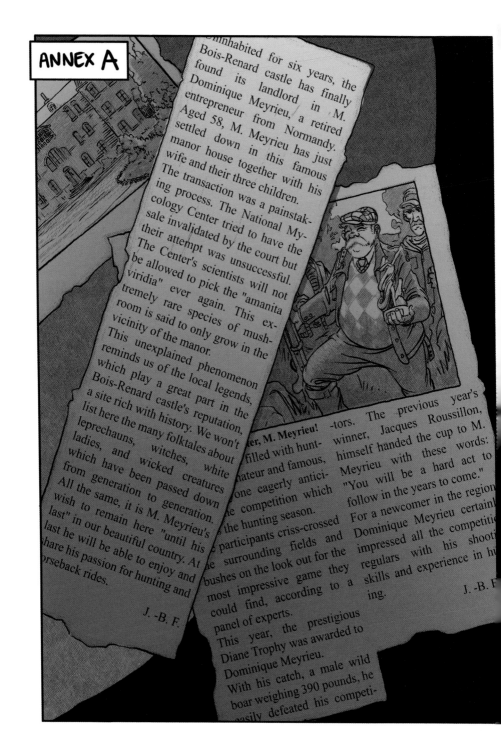

...inhabited for six years, the Bois-Renard castle has finally found its landlord in M. Dominique Meyrieu, a retired entrepreneur from Normandy. Aged 58, M. Meyrieu has just settled down in this famous manor house together with his wife and their three children. The transaction was a painstaking process. The National Mycology Center tried to have the sale invalidated by the court but their attempt was unsuccessful. The Center's scientists will not be allowed to pick the "amanita viridia" ever again. This extremely rare species of mushroom is said to only grow in the vicinity of the manor.

This unexplained phenomenon reminds us of the local legends, which play a great part in the Bois-Renard castle's reputation, a site rich with history. We won't list here the many folktales about leprechauns, witches, white ladies, and wicked creatures which have been passed down from generation to generation. All the same, it is M. Meyrieu's wish to remain here "until his last" in our beautiful country. At last he will be able to enjoy and share his passion for hunting and horseback rides.

J.-B. F.

...er, M. Meyrieu! ...filled with hunt- ...ateur and famous, ...one eagerly antici- ...e competition which ...the hunting season. ...participants criss-crossed ...e surrounding fields and bushes on the look out for the most impressive game they could find, according to a panel of experts.

This year, the prestigious Diane Trophy was awarded to Dominique Meyrieu. With his catch, a male wild boar weighing 390 pounds, he easily defeated his competi-

...tors. The previous year's winner, Jacques Roussillon, himself handed the cup to M. Meyrieu with these words: "You will be a hard act to follow in the years to come." For a newcomer in the region Dominique Meyrieu certainl impressed all the competiti regulars with his shooti skills and experience in hu ing.

J.-B. F

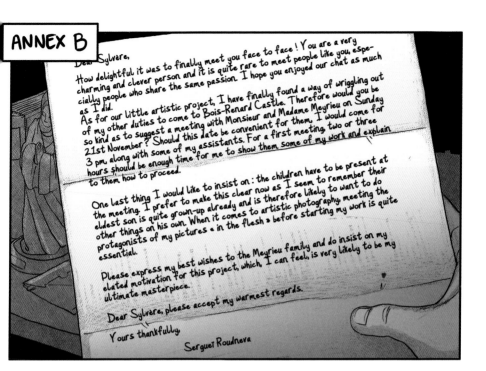

Dear Sylvère,

How delightful it was to finally meet you face to face! You are a very charming and clever person and it is quite rare to meet people like you, especially people who share the same passion. I hope you enjoyed our chat as much as I did.

As for our little artistic project, I have finally found a way of wriggling out of my other duties to come to Bois-Renard Castle. Therefore would you be so kind as to suggest a meeting with Monsieur and Madame Meyrieu on Sunday 21st November? Should this date be convenient for them, I would come for 3 pm, along with some of my assistants. For a first meeting, two or three hours should be enough time for me to show them some of my work and explain to them how to proceed.

One last thing I would like to insist on: the children have to be present at the meeting. I prefer to make this clear now as I seem to remember their eldest son is quite grown-up already and is therefore likely to want to do other things on his own. When it comes to artistic photography, meeting the protagonists of my pictures « in the flesh » before starting my work is quite essential.

Please express my best wishes to the Meyrieu family and do insist on my elated motivation for this project, which, I can feel, is very likely to be my ultimate masterpiece.

Dear Sylvère, please accept my warmest regards.

Yours thankfully

Serguei Roudneva

Sylvère,

I have just been to my drama rehearsal. I should be back by 7 pm. Could you please ask Blandine to clear some space in the attic? It hasn't been done for six months and we may need the space should the photographer ask us to move some of the furniture or some of our objects that may be in the way. Please also ask her to sweep the secret staircase of our bedroom. I went there this morning and I really thought I was going to choke with all the dust. I have put the key back under the little doll. In case she might have forgotten, the switch is on the skirting board under the bedside table.

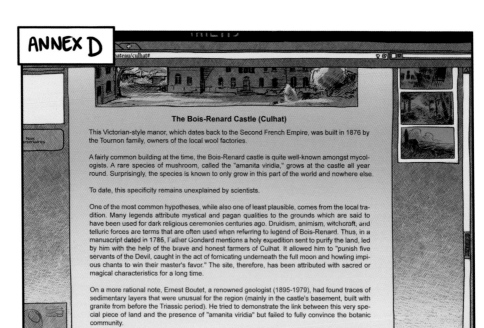

The Bois-Renard Castle (Culhat)

This Victorian-style manor, which dates back to the Second French Empire, was built in 1876 by the Tournon family, owners of the local wool factories.

A fairly common building at the time, the Bois-Renard castle is quite well-known amongst mycologists. A rare species of mushroom, called the "amanita viridia," grows at the castle all year round. Surprisingly, the species is known to only grow in this part of the world and nowhere else.

To date, this specificity remains unexplained by scientists.

One of the most common hypotheses, while also one of least plausible, comes from the local tradition. Many legends attribute mystical and pagan qualities to the grounds which are said to have been used for dark religious ceremonies centuries ago. Druidism, animism, witchcraft, and telluric forces are terms that are often used when referring to legend of Bois-Renard. Thus, in a manuscript dated in 1785, Father Gondard mentions a holy expedition sent to purify the land, led by him with the help of the brave and honest farmers of Culhat. It allowed him to "punish five servants of the Devil, caught in the act of fornicating underneath the full moon and howling impious chants to win their master's favor." The site, therefore, has been attributed with sacred or magical characteristics for a long time.

On a more rational note, Ernest Boutet, a renowned geologist (1895-1979), had found traces of sedimentary layers that were unusual for the region (mainly in the castle's basement, built with granite from before the Triassic period). He tried to demonstrate the link between this very special piece of land and the presence of "amanita viridia" but failed to fully convince the botanic community.

HOW TO USE ENTROPY SIGNS IN SACRED THAUMATURGY

Over the centuries, so many have wanted to master the power of the Great Sign through a ritual of growth in order to become immortal, omniscient, or omnipotent. Most of them have perished in their endeavor. Success is yet achievable as the Sign is real, the Sign is powerful, and the Sign is divine in its essence.

The three other main elements of this ritual are well documented - the Site, the Receptacle, and the Duplicator. Making them coincide with the Sign, however, is not enough to ensure a successful ritual. Ultimately harmony in time is more important than harmony in space.

It is the precise moment that makes the magic of the ritual possible. If the Sign is in contact with the Receptacle, which must be a pure virgin human being at the very moment when the words

of power, Nego Chlarrisskia Karvala are uttered by the inceptor, at the end of the incantation, then the divine essence of the Sign will be transmitted and the ritual will commence. Be warned: do not touch the wrists of the Receptacle with the Sign, as they are that of the Guarding divinities who have always seen to it that the magic was absolved. This so as to keep mankind in its state of endless servitude.

In order to use the Sign to achieve a ritual of growth, another key element is its composition. The Sign is served by ostentation and shines with great mystical fires when it is in contact with life. Some ambitious minds in past centuries depicted them on frescoes or engraved them on the hilts of their swords, or on the mantle of a familial hearth.

When they were aptly instructed and sanctified, while these Signs proved efficient they could not contribute to the success of a ritual of growth. Ideally, the Great Sign grows and expands when it is engraved on a piece of jewelry, a locket with a chain worn close to one's heart for example. A ring, an earring, or even a bracelet would also suffice.

WRITE DOWN THE CODE "NEGO" IN YOUR NOTES.

THE SIGIL, THE SITE, THE RECEPTACLE, THE DUPLICATOR: I HAVE BROUGHT THEM TOGETHER AT LAST. IT IS NEARLY TIME. YEARS WASTED, HUNTING FOR ONE OF THE ENTROPY SIGILS IN RUSSIA AND EASTERN EUROPE. AS IF THESE ARTIFACTS COULDN'T BE FOUND IN MY OWN COUNTRY. PURE VANITY.

MY DEAR DISCIPLE, HERE IS THE LESSON TO BE LEARNED FROM ALL OF THIS: INTUITION IS MERELY AN ILLUSION CREATED BY OUR FEELINGS. IT IS THEREFORE UNRELIABLE.

IN THE END, THE SIGIL WAS IN FRANCE, RIGHT WHERE MY OWN MASTER HAD BROUGHT ME UP, TRAINED ME, AND SHOWING ME THE PATH OF THE STARS. ITS WAS TO BE EXPECTED, THE SIGIL WAS IN THE HANDS OF ONE OF THE GUARDIANS, OUR SWORN ENEMIES. HAS ANYONE EVER TAKEN POWER EASILY?

YET I BELIEVE IN THE WORTHLESSNESS OF OUR ENDER, AND SUCCESS OF OUR QUEST MANY FACTIONS ARE CLEARLY IN OUR FAVOR, PARTICULARLY THIS REMARKABLE CLOSENESS BETWEEN THE ENTROPY SIGIL AND THE ANCESTRAL SITE. THE GUARDIAN LIVES JUST WERE MILES FROM THE BOSOM OF BOIS-EDWARD. ABOUT MY MISTAKE, AS YOU WERE CORRECT IN SUGGESTING THESE MANY YEARS AGO THAT THE GUARDIANS HAS PURPOSELY SETTLED DOWN NEAR THIS PLACE OF POWER. BUT I DO NOT REGRET CUTTING OFF YOUR HANDS TO PUNISH YOU FOR YOUR INSOLENCE. THAT WAS A LESSON IN HUMILITY YOU WOULD BE WISE TO REMEMBER IF ONE DAY YOU WISH TO TAKE OVER FROM ME.

IN TRUTH, THIS GUARDIAN SEEMS QUITE WEAK WHEN COMPARED TO HIS PREDECESSORS. I HAVE BEEN WATCHING HIM FOR SEVERAL WEEKS AND HE BELIEVES, AS IF HE IS UNAWARE OF HIS HERITAGE, LET ALONE THE SIGIL HE IS RESPONSIBILITY, AS IF HE HAD POWER TO FACE US. HE CHARGED WITH PROTECTING. HE HAS NO UNDERSTANDING OF WHAT IS AT STAKE. HE DOES, HE HAS PAY UNDERSTANDINGS OF WHAT HIS SPAWN IS TO SUSPECTS NOTHING, LEAST OF ALL THE PART HE IS TO PLAY.

THE RECEPTACLE! I CAN STILL HEAR YOUR WHINING, YOUR PRETENTIOUS IMPERTINENCE, WHICH GRATES ON ME. "NEVER WILL A GIRL HER AGE BE ABLE TO BEAR SUCH A RITUAL. EVERY GREAT BOOK INSISTS ON THE RELIABILITY OF THE RECEPTACLE: AN ACOLYTE, WEAK OR SICKLY MIND." A MISERABLE SECOND-CLASS CORRUPT! DO YOU REALLY THINK THE BLOOD DAUGHTER OF A GUARDIAN WOULD HAVE A WEAK MIND?

AS FOR THE DUPLICATOR, I HAVE POSSESSED IT FOR AGES, SINCE MY MASTER TRUSTED IT INTO MY CARE. LONG AGO, SO LONG AGO THAT I CAN'T EVEN REMEMBER THE EXACT DATE. I HAVE GROWN

MORE POWERFUL UNDER ITS INFLUENCE. MY BEING, MY BODY, MY SPIRIT, AND MY SOUL ARE ONE WITH IT. BUT IT IS DANGEROUS. WHEN THE GREATER RITUAL WAS BEGUN FIVE DAYS AGO, I COULD FEEL IT RESONATE WITH UNTOLD POWER. SHOULD IT CONNECT TOO CLOSELY, IT WOULD SPELL FAILURE FOR OUR ULTIMATE GOAL. THAT'S WHY I HAVE PUT IT SOMEWHERE SAFE OUTSIDE THE MANOR, SOMEWHERE NO ONE WILL EVER FIND IT OR EVEN UNWITTINGLY BRING IT BACK. BUT AS SOON AS THE RITUAL HAS BEEN EXECUTED, THE DUPLICATOR WILL MAKE THIS MAGIC STRONGER, AND THE RESULT WILL BE GREATER THAN WE COULD EVER HAVE HOPED FOR.

THE DUPLICATOR IS THEREFORE ESSENTIAL TO ANY GREAT PRIEST OF OUR ORDER. WHEN YOU ARE READY AND YOU HAVE EARNED IT, WE WILL LOCATE AND FOR YOU AND YOUR PERCEPTION OF THE DARK ARCANE MAGIES WILL CHANGE COMPLETELY.

YET ANOTHER THING YOU COULD NOT FULLY GRASP IS WHY WE PREPARED THE SITE SO EARLY BEFORE THE RITUAL WOULD BE COMPLETED. CHANTING AND PRAYING AND COMMUNING WITH THE DARKNESS.

YOU SEE, THE SITE WAS LOST SOME OF ITS POTENCY. THE MYSTICAL VIBRATIONS NEEDED TO WAKE UP THE TELLURIC FORCES ARE WEAK AND THIN, NO DOUBT DUE TO PROLONGED CONTACT WITH THIS PEDESTRIAN FAMILY AND THEIR THREE CHILDREN, THEIR PATHETIC SERVANTS, AND THAT DAMNED BUTLER WHO IS MORE ZEALOUSLY RELIGIOUS THAN A CATHOLIC PATRIARCH. KILLING THEM ALL WAS NECESSARY, BUT HOW COULD THE MOTHER ESCAPE? YOU SAID NONE OF OUR BROTHERS HAD SEEN HER WHEN WE BEGAN THE PURGE, BUT ALL OF THE VEHICLES WERE ACCOUNTED FOR IN THIS HENHOUSE. SHE WOULD NOT HAVE REALLY HAS BEEN IN HIDING OVER THE PAST FEW DAYS, A NECRO-RESANATING MANIFESTATION (A BYPRODUCT OF THE RITUAL) WILL GET THE BETTER OF HER SANITY. THE PLANTS IN THE GARDEN WERE THE FIRST TO ROT, AND A KIND OF PREMATURE RESONATE WITH A KIND OF HAVE NOTICED ARTICLES OF PREMATURE RESONATE WITH A KIND OF EAGER AWARENESS. SOON, THE EXTRA MAUVE WILL HAVE CHANGES BUT WE WILL NO LONGER BE HERE. AS FOR THE MOONLIKE LARVA WHICH PROWLS ABOUT IN THE WOODS, IT ONLY COMES OUT AT NIGHT AND IS EASILY AVOIDED.

THESE FEW MUTATIONS, DISTORTIONS, AND ABOMINATIONS WILL ONLY BE WORTH A FEW TROUBLES COMPARED TO THE MATTER OF POWER THAT WE ARE ON THE VERGE OF UNLOCKING.

I AM THE PROPHET. IN ANCIENT GREECE, THIS TITLE MEANT THE MOUTHPIECE OF THE GODS. IF YES, THE TRUE GODS HAVE A MESSAGE TO DELIVER TO MANKIND, AND I AM HERE TO SPREAD ACROSS THIS DOOMED AND FORSAKEN WORLD.

Wednesday 13th November

Hubert's snake has escaped to the corridor yet again. Dominique barely told him off. He didn't even dare deprive him of his pocket money! He's so soft! I've known that for a long time of course. But after nearly 20 years with him, I've come to realise he after all has grown old...

Barcelona... Another moment's adventure, taking me through the Net, to find the best bargain for a trip. All he cares about is his travelling, his animals, or at a pinch his house or his cars for which he lives. As for us, his children, he doesn't mind spending his money. As for his children, he doesn't listen, even seem to notice we're there, he hears us but doesn't listen to us, as if we were pieces of furniture. Anyway, needless to go on and on about it. I must have written about it at least ten times.

Friday 15th November

For my birthday (42 already, so unpleasant!), the crew have given me a lovely present; a vestal's outfit for next year's play. After considering me as one of those conscious bourgeois (they thought I was from Paris...), they seem to have accepted me and it feels good to be with them, as I steed dress suit of a family. Besides, this Ancient Greece usual charmer... « How elegant Guillaume, being his usual charmer... You look like Eurydice from the Underworld. »

I about I looked Eurydice up to understand what he meant and I have to say it was a compliment. Anyway, it's typically the kind of chat-up line he would come up with it's his many actresses. All the same, it's always nice to hear.

Tuesday 19th November

Next Sunday the crew is organising a get-together with all the members of the association which is quite good timing for me as I said to Solange that he could confirm the appointment with that great Russian photographer. I'm stuck as the more as it was my idea in the first place... Famous as the man is, we can't even book another date. All I'll just have to forget about my pride, and ask Guillaume after the rehearsal tonight if we can postpone the meal until a later date. It would be such a shame to miss it, as it's the first time something is organised by the crew outside the show.

Wednesday 20th November

God, please forgive me. When he looked me in the eyes, I don't know what is happening to me. He took my hands, looking all serious, and gently hypnotised me. I couldn't do anything, looking me in the eyes. They are so big... and so dark they were primitive, flesh, how much he desired me... and so dark they were that was as if I had been waiting for someone to look at me that manner, regardless of my body. I filed it was. Oh, Lord, what am I ready of my rank age or physical appearance, whilst all the actors were laying me on the table, wanting to look at me in dusting on the right behind me, wanting to look at me in dusting on the other side of the curtain, I would have given...

How can ask anything so light then he came closer to me, Solange, kiss but I could feel his warm lips, his hand resting on my neck. It flesh of his moustache against my skin, while seating. It seemed so eager, burning Oh, my god! Please don't let this happen to me...

He just said: Sure, let's just postpone it till next week. Then he came closer to me, Solange, kiss but I could feel his warm lips, his hand resting on my neck. It was a light...

Saturday 23rd November

I hate him. Bitterly. How could he do this, believe so lightly smile, which had happened. A married, respectable woman. Since then, he acts as if nothing had happened. To express anything for his malicious look I haven't been able to sleep for three nights, forgotten anything I don't know what to do. If I try to talk to him and ask him, to apologize, or just express my anger at him and ask is that possible? I will just find myself into his arms, doing that photo shoot. Besides, tomorrow, we are able to resist and I won't be those sleepless nights, I am going to look terrible. With all

Achievements

If you've just finished your adventure in 280, congratulations! You've succeeded in completing your mission and rescuing your daughter. There are many ways to reach your goal, some requiring more heroism, luck, and intelligence than others. Check the following list of achievements to calculate your ultimate score.

Kill the cultist with a gun without being wounded **+2**

Kill the cultist with the shurikens without being wounded **+2**

Find the newspaper clippings in the first secret room **+1**

Find the letter the Prophet wrote to Sylvère **+1**

Find the burnt note and the yellow key **+1**

Discover the right combination to gain entry to the second secret room **+3**

Find the bottle of cognac in the cellar **+1**

Kill the cultist with the blades without being wounded **+2**

Arrive in time to save Clovis **+4**

Discover the secret staircase **+3**

Read the internet article about the manor **+1**

Find the diary **+1**

Find the Prophet's personal notes **+1**